Ranches and Farms Across America

by Anika Brennan

Harcourt
SCHOOL PUBLISHERS

Cover, ©CREATAS IMAGES/PunchStock; p.3, ©Willard R. Culver/National Geographic/Getty Images; p.4, (tl) ©MARESA PRYOR/Animals Animals, (tr) ©PhotoDisc/PunchStock, (bl) ©Tom Edwards/Visuals Unlimited, (br) ©Walt Anderson/Visuals Unlimited; p.5, ©Steve Bly/Riser/Getty Images; p.6, ©Tyler Stableford/The Image Bank/Getty Images; p.7, ©Andy Sacks/Stone/Getty Images; p.8, ©VIRGINIA NEEFUS/Animals Animals; p.9, ©Jupiter Images; p.10, ©Andrew Sacks/STONE/Getty Images; p.11, ©Mula Eshet/Flock of sheep, New Zealand, Pacific/Getty Images; p.12, ©Hans Reinhard/zefa/Corbis; p.13, ©Holt Studios International Ltd/Alamy; p.14, ©William Albert Allard/National Geographic/Getty Images.

Printed in China

ISBN 10: 0-15-350230-4
ISBN 13: 978-0-15-350230-9

P9-CSV-565

Ordering Options
ISBN 10: 0-15-349939-7 (Grade 4 ELL Collection)
ISBN 13: 978-0-15-349939-5 (Grade 4 ELL Collection)
ISBN 10: 0-15-357289-2 (package of 5)
ISBN 13: 978-0-15-357289-0 (package of 5)

1 2 3 4 5 6 7 8 9 10 985 12 11 10 09 08 07 06

All across America, there are wide-open lands. Open land is called a prairie. Prairie land has rolling hills with tall grasses, small bushes, and few trees. This land is good for raising different kinds of animals. Ranches are farms where these animals are raised.

Many different kinds of animals are raised on ranches. Cattle are raised on ranches. Cattle are large animals with horns and hooves. Female cattle are called cows. Male cattle are called bulls.

There are many different colors of cattle. Some cattle are all brown. Other cattle have brown bodies and white heads. Others are black with big, white spots. Cattle have different sized horns. Some horns are short and curved. Other cattle, such as the longhorn cattle, have long, beautiful horns!

Ranches have large, open pieces of land where the cattle live. This land is called a range. A range is closed in with fences. Ranges can be as large as many football fields put together. A range is covered in grass, which the cattle eat. Cattle travel in large groups called herds. Workers ride on horses around the herds to keep the cattle together. The workers might also use dogs to help keep the cattle together.

The land on some cattle ranches is divided
into smaller parts called pastures. Pastures are
closed in with fences, too. Cattle are kept inside
the pastures. Some cattle are kept in smaller areas
with fences. Here, cattle workers feed the cattle
hay, which is grass that has been cut and dried.
Hay is stored in large bundles called bales. Cattle
also eat grains, such as corn. Cattle usually get fed
once a day.

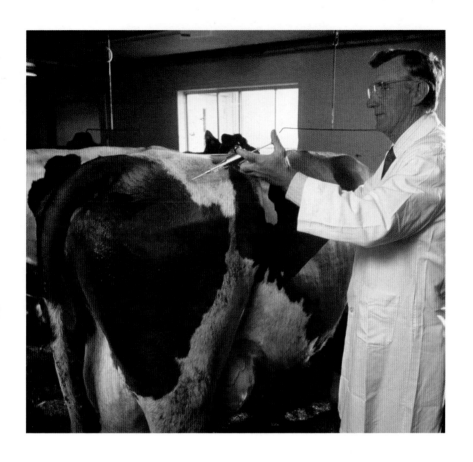

Work is hard on a cattle ranch. Cattle workers often get up before the sun rises. They must check to make sure that the cows are in good health. Special animal doctors called veterinarians visit the farms to check on the cattle. The veterinarians give the cattle shots so that the cattle do not get sick.

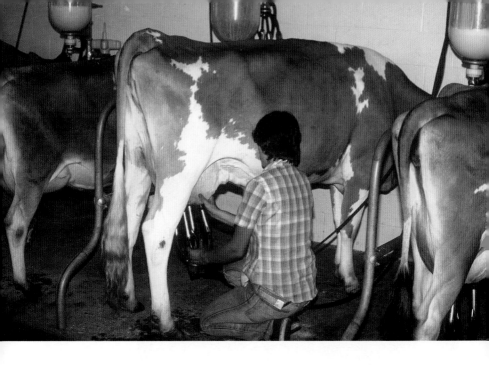

Some cattle are raised for their milk. These kinds of cattle are found on dairy farms. The milk comes from female cows. A female cow has body parts called udders. Milk comes from the udders. To get the milk, the cows are put into stalls. Then the cows' udders are hooked up to milking machines. The milk flows to a container.

A dairy cow is milked two or three times each day. Most dairy cows make about 12 gallons (45 l) of milk each day. Most dairy cows are milked every single day of the year! One dairy farm may have hundreds or even thousands of cows.

milk
cheese
butter
ice cream

Work is hard on a dairy farm, too. Dairy farmers also get up before the sun rises. They need to keep the cows' stalls clean. Then they turn on the milking machines. During the day, the dairy farmers check to make sure the milk machines are working and that the milk is not bad. Dairy farmers make sure the cows are healthy, too.

Some of the milk from a dairy farm may be sent to another place. Cheese, ice cream, yogurt, and other dairy products are made with the milk.

Pigs are other animals that are raised on farms. A pig is a fat animal with short legs and hooves. Pigs are kept in pastures on a pig farm, just like cattle. Sometimes pigs are raised inside buildings. Pigs eat corn and other grains, such as oats and wheat.

People think that pigs are dirty animals because they roll in the mud. This is not true. Pigs cannot sweat, so they roll in the mud to keep cool.

Sheep are also raised on farms. Sheep live in herds in fenced-in pastures. They eat grasses and leaves. Grown male sheep are called rams. Grown female sheep are called ewes. Baby sheep are called lambs.

Sheep are woolly animals with hooves. During the winter, the sheep grow very thick wool coats. The wool is sheared, or cut, off the sheep each year at the beginning of summer. Shearing does not hurt the sheep. The wool is made into yarn. Yarn is then made into clothes, such as sweaters and socks or cloth.

Chickens are raised on poultry farms. Chickens are often raised for their eggs. Chickens cannot fly long distances like most birds can. Chickens have a red flap on their heads called a comb. The male chicken is called a rooster. The female chicken is called a hen. The hens lay the eggs. The hens live in large buildings called henhouses. Hens eat different kinds of grains.

The hens lay eggs in special nests on many poultry farms. The eggs drop through the nests and fall onto a moving belt. The moving belt drops the eggs into a large bin. The eggs are checked to see if they are cracked. The good eggs are washed and put into egg cartons. Then the eggs get shipped to stores.

It is hard work to raise animals on farms and ranches. A farm or a ranch must have the latest tools and machines to care for the animals. People who run the ranches or farms must make enough money to keep the ranches or farms going.

Ranches and farms are found all across America. Many cattle ranches are in large states such as Montana, Kansas, Texas, and Arizona. Dairy farms and poultry farms can be found in just about any state.

Ranches and farms are important. People get many of the foods they eat from these ranches and farms. They also provide places for people to work all across America.

Scaffolded Language Development

ADJECTIVES Review adjectives with students by pointing out examples in the book, such as *large* and *beautiful.* Remind students that adjectives are words that describe nouns. Read each adjective in the word bank. Model the meaning of each word by showing the motion of "rolling" hills with your hands, drawing a "curved" shape on the board, and so on. Have students chorally read each sentence below. Then have students choose one or two adjectives to add to the sentence, and have students reread the new sentences.

Word Bank: rolling, curved, wide-open, woolly, thick, important

1. The land has hills.
2. The bull has horns.
3. The pastures are spaces.
4. The sheep have fur.
5. Farms are a part of life.

Social Studies

Farms Everywhere Explain to students that there are farms in every state. Have students research and make a list of what the farms in your state produce.

School-Home Connection
What Farmers Do Have students talk to family members about what farmers do. Encourage students to use information from this book in their conversation.

Word Count: 938